This book is a gift

To:

_____

From:

_____

Date:

_____

Every day with Jesus

christian art kids

Open Letter to Children

You are special, God chose you to be His child.

   Every Day with Jesus will teach you what the Bible says about being God's child. It will also teach you how to become more like Jesus.

   Each reading will inspire you to do the following:

 **?** Think) about some important things you will learn.

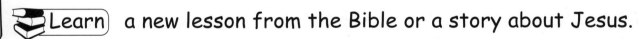 Learn) a new lesson from the Bible or a story about Jesus.

 Pray) to Jesus every day.

   Friends may change, but Jesus is a friend who will be with you all the time. I hope this book will help you to get to know your Bible and Jesus in a wonderful way.

Your friend and Jesus' friend,
Paul J. Loth, Ed.D.

Contents

Answering Our Friends

Luke 5:27-39

 **Think**

When was the last time someone asked you to explain your actions? What did you say?

 **Learn**

The Bible tells us we should act like Jesus. God sent the Holy Spirit to help us.

Jesus did not act like other people. People asked Him why He acted different.

We should act like Jesus. Our friends will ask why we act that way. We can tell them. It is because we love Jesus.

 Pray

Dear Jesus, make me brave enough to act like You.

Honor Christ and let him be
the Lord of your life. Always be
ready to give an answer when
someone asks you about your hope.

1 Peter 3:15

Doing Our Job

Acts 20:17-38

Think

When was the last time you had a job to do?

Learn

Jesus has a job for us. It is to tell our friends about Him. That is what Jesus wants us to do.

Paul told people about Jesus. Paul did his job. He told many people about Jesus.

Our job is to tell our friends about Jesus. It is up to them to trust in Him.

 Pray

Dear Jesus, please help me tell my friends about You.

I have told you everything that
God wants you to know.

Acts 20:27

Getting Help from God

John 16:7-15

Think

Have you told your friends why you believe in Jesus? What did they say?

Learn

Jesus sent us a helper. The helper is the Holy Spirit.

The Holy Spirit helps us. He helps when we talk to our friends. He will help us know what to say. He helps us tell them about Jesus.

We must ask the Holy Spirit for help. We do this by praying. The Holy Spirit will help us.

✝ Pray

Dear Jesus, may the Holy Spirit help me talk to a friend.

The Spirit will come and show the
people of this world the truth.
John 16:8

Getting Help from God in Prayer

Romans 8:26-28

 **Think**

Do you always know the right thing to say?

 **Learn**

Sometimes we don't know what to pray for. We need help.
God helps us remember what to pray for.
We need to listen to God when we pray. Then we will be sure to pray for the right things.

 Pray

Dear Jesus, help me to know what to pray for.

In certain ways we are weak,
but the Spirit is here to help us.
Romans 8:26

A Good Testimony

Acts 26

 **Think**

Have you ever told a friend about Jesus? What did you say?

 **Learn**

Paul knew about the Bible. He became a Christian. He told people about Jesus.

Paul told what Jesus did for him. He said that Jesus helped him each day.

We can tell our friends what Jesus does for us.

 **Pray**

Dear Jesus, what can I tell my friends that You have done for me? Please show me.

We cannot keep quiet about
what we have seen and heard.
Acts 4:20

Helping Jesus, Our Friend

Matthew 28:16-20; Mark 16:14-20

 **Think**

If your friends asked you to help them, what would you do? Why?

 **Learn**

Jesus is our best friend. We like to help our friends.

Jesus asked His friends to help Him. He told them to tell others about Him. They went all over the world. Jesus was pleased.

Jesus wants our help, too. We can tell people about Jesus.

 Pray

Dear Jesus, please show me whom I can tell about You this week.

Go and preach the good news
to everyone in the world.
Mark 16:15

Helping Our Friends Love Jesus

1 Corinthians 8

 **Think**

How do you help your friends?
Are your friends better or worse because of your friendship?

 **Learn**

In Paul's time there was a problem. People had different ideas about right and wrong.

What should they do?

Paul taught them a lesson. They were not to do anything that would hurt another person. If they kept this in mind they would know right from wrong.

This is still right.

✝ Pray

Dear Jesus, please show me how to help a friend walk closer to You.

> I am willing to put up with anything.
> Then God's special people will be saved.
> 2 Timothy 2:10

Letting the Bible Speak for Us

Acts 2:14-39; 13:13-41

 **Think**

How do you decide whom to believe when you and your friends disagree?
Is one of your friends always right?

Learn

Sometimes we do not know how to tell about Jesus. The disciples did. They told what the Bible said. It tells about Jesus.

Paul told people about Jesus. Paul knew verses from the Bible. The verses told about Jesus.

We can tell friends about Jesus. We can tell them what the Bible says. It tells about Jesus.

✝ Pray

Dear Jesus, please help me learn Bible verses to share with a friend.

My word . . . shall accomplish
what I please.
Isaiah 55:11, NKJV

Praying for Unsaved Friends

John 14-16

 **Think**

When was the last time you had trouble doing something?
Did you ask for help?

 **Learn**

We may need help telling our friends about Jesus. We can tell them what Jesus means to us. But they still do not trust in Jesus. God can help our friends to trust Jesus.

God can help our friends understand about Jesus. We can also help our friends. We can pray for them. It will help.

 Pray

Dear Jesus, please help my friends understand about You.

God is patient, because he wants
everyone to turn from sin.
2 Peter 3:9

Sharing Our Experiences

John 9:1-34

 **Think**

When something good happens to you, do you want to tell someone?
Whom do you tell?

 **Learn**

A man could not see. He had always been blind.

One day Jesus helped the man see. He was very happy.

He told the people what Jesus did for him.

We can tell our friends how Jesus helps us, too. This is how we share about Jesus.

✝ Pray

Dear Jesus, show me how to share ways You have helped me.

> All I know is that I used to be
> blind, but now I can see!
> John 9:25

Standing Up for God

Exodus 32; Acts 4-5

 **Think**

When has a friend stood up for you? How did you feel?

 **Learn**

Moses stood up for God. He spoke to the people. He said to worship only God. Peter told about Jesus. Some leaders told him to be quiet. But he was not. He stood up for Jesus.

We can stand up for Jesus, too. We can be like Moses and Peter.

 Pray

Dear Jesus, please help me to be strong and brave for You.

> If you tell others that you belong
> to me, I will tell my father in
> heaven that you are my followers.
>
> Matthew 10:32

Telling Our Friends We Love Them

John 13:34-35; Philippians 1:3-8; 1 Thessalonians 2:19-20

 **Think**

When was the last time someone told you they loved you? How did you feel?

 **Learn**

People can tell we love Jesus. We should be kind to one another. Then people will know that we love Jesus.

Paul did more than that. He told his friends he loved them. He showed them he loved them.

We should show our friends that we love them. God likes it when we love each other.

 Pray

Dear Jesus, please help me tell my friends I love them.

If you love each other, everyone
will know you are my disciples.
John 13:35

Using Our Opportunities

Acts 8:26-39

 **Think**

Have you ever had a chance to do something you really wanted to do? How did you feel?

 **Learn**

Philip saw a man reading the Bible. The man did not understand what he was reading. Philip told him. Philip told him about Jesus.

God gave Philip a chance. Philip used his chance. He told about Jesus. God gives us chances, too. We should be ready. We can tell what Jesus means to us.

 Pray

Dear Jesus, give me a chance to tell a friend about You.

We are telling you what we have
seen and heard, so that you may
share in this life with us.

1 John 1:3

Getting the
Point Across

Luke 11:5-8

 **Think**

When was the last time you had a hard time getting your point across to your parents? What did you do?

 **Learn**

God loves us. He wants what is best for us. He will give us what we need.

Jesus told a story: A friend knocks on our door. It is the middle of the night. "Let me borrow some food," he says. We say, "Go away." He keeps knocking. Finally, we get the food.

Jesus explained the story. If we would help a friend, God will surely give us what we need.

✝ Pray

Dear Jesus, please give me the faith to keep praying.

So I tell you to ask
and you will receive.

Luke 11:9

A Picture of a Prayer Warrior

Matthew 4:1-11; Luke 6:12-16; 22:39-46

Think

Whom do you know who prays a lot?
When does that person pray?

Learn

Jesus prayed about many things. He prayed about His friends. He prayed the night before He died.

Jesus asked God what to do. He listened to what God told Him. God helped Him do the right thing.

 **Pray**

Dear Jesus, help me pray every day this week.

> Never stop praying.
> 1 Thessalonians 5:17

A Picture Perfect Prayer

Luke 11:2-4

 **Think**

How do you learn something new?

 **Learn**

Jesus showed us how to pray. We can copy Him.

Jesus prayed the Lord's Prayer. This special prayer teaches us how to pray.

We should praise God. Next, ask Him to forgive our sins. Then we can ask God to help us.

 **Pray**

Dear Jesus, help me to learn how to pray.

> Morning, noon, and night, you
> hear my concerns and my complaints.
> Psalm 55:17

Pray and Believe

Matthew 21:20-22

 Think

Have you ever asked for something that you did not really believe you would get?

 Learn

God loves us. He will do what is best for us. When we ask God for things, we can believe this.

God will answer our prayers. Jesus said we must have faith. If we have faith, we can tell a mountain to move. It will move!

When we have faith, we can pray and God will answer us.

✚ Pray

Dear Jesus, let me have faith when I pray to You.

> If you have faith when you pray, you
> will be given whatever you ask for.
> Matthew 21:22

Pray, Do Not Worry

Matthew 6:25-34

? Think

Have you ever seen a bird starve to death? Why not?
Who takes care of the birds?

 Learn

God takes care of everything. He cares for all the birds. He cares for the flowers.

But God loves people even more. More than flowers. More than birds.

Jesus told us not to worry. God will take care of us. We just have to ask Him. Instead of worrying, we can pray. God knows everything we need. All we need to do is talk to Him.

✞ Pray

Dear Jesus, help me to not worry, but to trust You for all I need.

> Don't worry about anything,
> but pray for everything.
> Philippians 4:6

Prayer Works

Acts 12:1-19

 **Think**

When you really want something, what do you do?

 **Learn**

One day Peter was talking about Jesus. He was put in jail. The Christians loved Peter. They wanted to help him. What could they do?

They could pray. They asked God to help Peter. God heard their prayer. He sent angels. Peter was freed.

They learned a lesson. Prayer works!

✝ Pray

Dear Jesus, when I am worried, please help me remember to pray.

The prayer of an innocent
person is powerful.

James 5:16

Praying
for Others

Acts 20:17-38; Ephesians 6:18-20; Philippians 1:3-11

 **Think**

Have you ever wanted to help someone but did not know what to do?

What is the best way to help your friends?

 **Learn**

Paul asked people to pray for him. Paul prayed that God would help his friends live for God.

Paul said goodbye to his friends in Ephesus. Paul did something special with these friends. He prayed for them. He asked God to take care of them.

We can do that with our friends, too. The best way we can help our friends is to pray for them.

✝ Pray

Dear Jesus, I pray for all the friends on my prayer list. Please take care of them.

> Never give up praying.
> Colossians 4:2

Praying with Our Friends

Acts 1:9-26

? Think

When was the last time you prayed with someone else?
How was it different from praying alone?

 Learn

Jesus had gone to heaven. The disciples were together. They were in the upper room. Jesus told them to wait there.

What did they do while they waited? They prayed. Everyone prayed to God. They prayed together.

God wants us to pray together, too. We can pray with our friends. This is a good way for friends to show they care.

✝ Pray

Dear Jesus, please help me to pray with my friends this week.

> I want everyone everywhere to lift
> innocent hands toward heaven and pray.
>
> 1 Timothy 2:8

Thanking God in Prayer

Luke 18:35-42

 **Think**

When someone does something nice for you, what do you say? Why?

 **Learn**

Jesus healed a man who was blind. What do you think the man said? Right. He said thank You. He praised Jesus. This pleased Jesus.

God wants us to thank Him, too. When we pray, God answers our prayers. He wants us to remember to thank Him.

✝ Pray

Dear God, I thank You for Your love, and for all You give me.

It is wonderful to be grateful and
to sing your praises, LORD most high!
Psalm 92:1

Using Prayer to Praise God

Ephesians 1

 **Think**

Do you listen when someone prays in church?
Why do people pray out loud?

 **Learn**

The Psalms give praise to God. Many of the psalms are prayers to God.

God likes to hear that we love Him. We can tell Him that when we pray.

When we pray in church, we praise God. Church services are good times to praise God together.

 Pray

Dear God, You are good. You are great. Help me to praise You.

I will praise you each day
and always honor your name.
Psalm 145:2

Changing Our Reflections

James 1:21-26

Think

What do you see when you look in the mirror?

Learn

We should all read our Bibles. It shows us if we are obeying God.

Some people read the Bible. But they do not change. That is like looking in a mirror and forgetting what you see.

We should do what the Bible says. Then we are obeying God.

 Pray

Dear Jesus, please let me be changed by reading the Bible.

Obey God's message! Don't fool
yourselves by just listening to it.
James 1:22

Keeping God's Word

Psalm 119:11

 **Think**

Do you have trouble remembering important things?
How do you do it?

 **Learn**

We do not always have our Bible with us. How do we know
what it says? We can memorize parts of it. Then we can think
about it anytime.

David memorized the Bible. He did it so he would not sin.

We can do the same thing. The more we know, the more it
will help us.

 Pray

Dear Jesus, please help me learn Your word by heart.

I treasure your word above all else;
it keeps me from sinning against you.
Psalm 119:11

Learning About God

Acts 2:42, 17:10-13; Romans 10:1-4

 **Think**

How do you learn about God?
When was the last time you learned something about God?
What was it?

 **Learn**

Church is important. It is one place we learn about God. We learn what Jesus taught.

The first Christians were taught by the apostles. They taught from the Scriptures.

They taught what Jesus had said. The Christians wanted to learn more about God.

We learn from the Bible. We learn from prayer and songs.

✝ Pray

Dear God, please help me learn more about Jesus in church.

Make me wise enough to learn
what you have commanded.
Psalm 119:73

Letting the Bible Explain Itself

Luke 4:16-21; Acts 2:14-36; Galatians 4:21-31

 **Think**

What do you do if someone says something you do not understand?

 **Learn**

A verse may be hard to understand. We have all had this problem.

Here is something we can do. We can look for other verses on the same subject. Then we read them, too. This will help.

We may want to learn about prayer. So we read many verses. This will make it clearer.

✚ Pray

Dear Jesus, please give me understanding. Help me to know Your word.

Help me understand your teachings.
Psalm 119:27

Telling Us How to Live

2 Timothy 3:1-17

Think

How do you know what you are to do?
Who tells you the rules to follow?

Learn

Rules help us. They tell us how to live. Our rule book is the Bible.

Paul wanted to help Timothy know how to live. He told him to study the Bible. The Bible would help him know what to do.

The Bible will help us do the right thing too. Knowing it will help us know how to live for Christ.

 Pray

Dear Jesus, please help me to live as the Bible tells me.

> Your word to me, your
> servant, is like pure gold.
> Psalm 119:140

Telling Us What to Believe

2 Timothy 3

 **Think**

If you wanted to find out the truth, what would you do? How do you know whom to believe?

 **Learn**

Paul told Timothy to expect hard times. The years would be tough. Paul wanted Timothy to be ready.

Timothy had been taught the Bible. Paul wanted him to keep reading the Bible. Then he would know what was right. The Bible would tell him what to believe.

We learn the same way.

Pray

Dear Jesus, when I am unsure about what to believe, help me find the answer in the Bible.

> I will take pleasure in your laws
> and remember your word.
> Psalm 119:16

Being a Giver in the Church

Acts 4:32-37

? Think

Tell about a time you gave something to someone.
How did you feel?

Learn

Jesus watched people give. One lady gave two coins. Jesus said, "She gave more than the others. She gave all she had."

We can give to God. We can give at church.

Some people are good at giving. They help the church. We should be givers, too.

✞ Pray

Dear Jesus, please help me give to others.

God loves people who love to give.
2 Corinthians 9:7

Being a Helper in the Church

Acts 6:1-7

 **Think**

Whom do you know who always helps others?

 **Learn**

The apostles needed help. They chose some helpers. Now they had more time to tell about Jesus.

Helping is easy for some people. All of us should try to help. Jesus would like that.

 Pray

Dear Jesus, please show me how to help someone at church.

Serve each other with love.
Galatians 5:13

Being a Leader in the Church

Romans 12:8; Ephesians 4:11-16

 **Think**

Do your friends always seem to follow what one person wants?

 **Learn**

Leaders in the Bible help others follow God. Jesus was the best leader of all.

God gives the church people to lead it.

Leaders help us do the right thing.

Our church has leaders. They help us serve God. We can be leaders, too.

✝ Pray

Dear Jesus, show me how I can be a leader right now.

> Christ chose some of us to be apostles, prophets, missionaries, pastors, and teachers.
> Ephesians 4:11-12

Being a Teacher

Romans 12:3-8; James 3:1

Think

Who taught you about God?
What special teachers do you know in the church?

Learn

People in the church teach us about God. We can teach our friends about God, too.

James said teachers should teach right things. They should be careful to teach God's truth.

God gave teachers to help us. They help us learn about God.

✝ Pray

Dear Jesus, thank You for those who teach me about You and Father God.

I want you to tell these same things to followers who can be trusted to tell others.

2 Timothy 2:2

Being an Encourager

Acts 4:36-37; 14:21-15:35

 **Think**

Whom do you know who encourages you?

 **Learn**

Barnabas was Paul's friend. He encouraged Paul. He made Paul feel better.

Barnabas did a good job. He was an encourager. We can encourage our friends. Our friends will feel better. We will feel good, too.

✝ Pray

Dear Jesus, please help me to be good at making people feel better.

Encourage and help each other.
1 Thessalonians 5:11

The Church Is Family

1 Corinthians 12:12-31

Think

How many members do you have in your family? How does your family take care of each other?

Learn

The church is like our body. Our body has many parts. Each part is different. But each part is important. The church is God's family.

Our family is like our body. Each of us has a job to do. We have a job to do in the church, too. We help each other. This is what it means to be in God's family.

 Pray

Dear Jesus, please help me to serve my church family.

> There are many of us, but we each
> are part of the body of Christ.
>
> Romans 12:5

Giving to God

Luke 21:1-4

Think

Do you give an offering at church? Why?

Learn

God is happy when we give to Him. It shows that we love Him.

Once Jesus watched people give offerings. A poor woman gave two small coins. Jesus was pleased. She gave all she had. Others gave what they did not need. The poor woman loved Jesus.

We can give offerings too. This shows that we love God. This pleases God.

✝ Pray

Dear Jesus, please help me to know what offering to give at church next Sunday.

> You will be blessed in every way, and you will be able to keep on being generous.
>
> 2 Corinthians 9:11

Listening to God

---

1 Samuel 3:1-10

? Think

Have you ever tried talking with someone who doesn't answer? Did you have trouble?

 Learn

Samuel was a young boy. He worked in the temple. Samuel heard God speak to him.

Samuel listened. God told Samuel all the plans He had for him.

God will talk to us, too. He calls us inside where only we can hear Him. The next time that happens, we should listen carefully.

✝ Pray

Dear Jesus, this week, help me listen to what You say.

Listen, my people, while I,
the LORD, correct you!
Psalm 81:8

Worshiping God Through Music

Psalm 150

 **Think**

What songs do you like to sing at church?
How do you think God feels when you sing songs about Him?

 **Learn**

King David wrote songs. He wrote about God. People sang these songs in worship. They used them to praise God.

God enjoys it when we sing. Many songs use words from the Bible. The choir sings. Instruments play. Everyone sings to God. God likes that.

We can worship God with music. God will listen.

![Pray] **Pray**

Dear Jesus, thank You for the joy of singing to You!

Shout praises to the LORD! Sing
him a new song of praise when
his loyal people meet.

Psalm 149:1

Worshiping Together

Psalm 147-149

 **Think**

Do you like to do things alone or with others? Why?

 **Learn**

God wants us to worship Him.

We do not worship God by ourselves. We do it with other people.

It is good to worship God with our friends. We can help each other. It is good to have friends to help us worship God.

✝ Pray

Dear God, make me glad to worship You with others!

> When your people meet, you will
> fill my heart with your praises, LORD.
> Psalm 22:25

Attendance Is Required

Acts 2:40-47

Think

Is there something that you have to attend? Do you like to go?

Learn

It is hard to be a Christian. Jesus knew it would be. That is why Jesus gave us churches.

The first Christians spent a lot of time together. They learned about God. They talked with each other. They prayed. They sang hymns.

We should spend time in church. It is good to be with others who believe as we do. We can help each other learn.

 Pray

Dear Jesus, thank You for giving me my church.

Some people have gotten out of
the habit of meeting for worship,
but we must not do that.
Hebrews 10:25

The Battle Is the Lord's

2 Chronicles 20

 **Think**

Has anyone else ever taken care of one of your problems? What happened?

 **Learn**

Israel was fighting a strong enemy They were scared. They prayed about it. "Go out and fight," God told them. "I have already won the battle for you."

So Israel fought. And they won!

God helps us every day, too. When we have a problem, God will help us. He will take care of us. What could be better than having God on our side?

✚ Pray

Dear Jesus, please help me with my problems. Help me know that You take care of me.

> The battle is not yours, but God's.
> *2 Chronicles 20:15,* NKJV

Doing Our Best for Jesus

Matthew 5:16; 1 Corinthians 10:31

 **Think**

What are some jobs you have done in the last week?
Did you do your best?

 **Learn**

Paul always did his best. He studied hard. He worked hard. He told people about Jesus. People knew he loved God.

We do all things to the glory of God.

We should always do our best. Then people will know we love God.

✝ Pray

Dear Jesus, please help me to do my best on the job.

Make your light shine, so that
others will see the good that you do
and will praise your Father in heaven.

Matthew 5:16

Enjoying God

Genesis 1; Luke 18:15-17

Think

When was the last time you enjoyed spending time with someone?

Learn

God wanted friends. So God made human beings. They enjoyed each other.

Children enjoyed being with Jesus. They had a good time together.

We can have a good time with God, too. We can enjoy God.

✝ Pray

Dear Jesus, please help me spend more time with You.

> So Jesus called the children over to him and said, "Let the children come to me!"
> Luke 18:16

Following God's Plan

Genesis 12:21-22

 **Think**

When you play with your friends, who decides what to do?

 **Learn**

God had a plan. He told Abraham and Sarah they would have a child.

God gave them a son. He was named Isaac. They had followed God's plan. This pleased God.

We need to follow God's plan, too.

 Pray

Dear God, do You have a plan for me to follow right now?

> But what the LORD has planned
> will stand forever.
> Psalm 33:11

Following Jesus

Matthew 4:18-22; John 13:1-20

 **Think**

Whom do you admire? Do you try to copy that person?

 **Learn**

Jesus had some helpers. They were His disciples. They followed Him.

Jesus taught them how to act. He taught by example. Jesus served others. He taught them to serve others.

We can follow Jesus, too. We will learn how to act. This will help us be like Jesus. This will please Jesus.

Dear Jesus, I want to live the way You lived. I need Your help.

Always live as God's holy people should.
1 Peter 1:15

Keeping God on Our Minds

Colossians 3:1-4

 **Think**

What do you think about when you're doing nothing else?

 **Learn**

Paul was in prison. He was still happy. How could that be?

Paul wrote letters while he was in prison. He explained why he was happy. He was thinking about Jesus. This made him happy.

This will work for us, too. We need to keep our minds on Jesus. Our problems won't seem so bad.

Pray

Dear Jesus, help me to keep my mind on You.

Think about what is up there,
not about what is here on earth.
Colossians 3:2

Keeping Our Minds on Good Things

Philippians 4

Think

What do you like to think about? Does what you think about affect how you act?

Learn

Christians in the early church had problems. People were mad at them. They were put into jail. Some were killed.

These were big problems. They thought about them all the time. It made it hard to do the right things.

Paul told the Christians to think about good things. Their minds would be filled with good things. They would be much happier.

 **Pray**

Dear Jesus, please help me think about good things this week.

Keep your minds on whatever is true,
pure, right, holy, friendly, and proper.
Philippians 4:8

Knowing God's Will

Psalm 119:105

 **Think**

What is the best way to find out what someone is thinking?

 **Learn**

We want to obey God. But how can we know what God wants us to do? We learn what to do when we pray and listen to Him. We listen by reading the Bible.

The Bible "is a lamp to my feet and light to my path." It will show us God's will.

We should read the Bible and pray to God. This will help us know God's will.

 **Pray**

Dear Jesus, please help me read my Bible every day.

Your word is a lamp that
gives light wherever I walk.
Psalm 119:105

Looking at Jesus

Matthew 14:22-33

 **Think**

When have you been somewhere very high in the sky? Were you scared?

 **Learn**

Peter saw Jesus walking on the water.

Jesus called, "Come." Peter was able to walk on the water, too. He was looking at Jesus. But Peter looked away from Jesus. He started to sink. Jesus saved him.

When Peter stopped looking at Jesus, he sank.

We should look at Jesus, too. Then we can do great things.

 Pray

Dear Jesus, when I am scared, please help me think of You.

> We must keep our eyes on Jesus, who leads us and makes our faith complete.
>
> Hebrews 12:2

Loving God

Mark 12:28-34; John 14:21-24

 **Think**

How do you treat people you love?
How do you know that people love you?

 **Learn**

Loving God is important. We should love Him with all our hearts.

If we love God, we will obey Him. The disciples loved God. They wanted to obey Him.

We love God, too. We want Him to be happy. We make God happy by obeying Him. This shows we love God.

✝ Pray

Dear Jesus, what have I done to show You that I love You?

> If anyone loves me, they will obey me.
> John 14:23

Making God Number One

Mark 10:17-22

Think

Who is your favorite friend? What does that mean?

Learn

A rich man asked a question: "What do I need to do to be saved?"

"What does the Bible say?" Jesus asked.

"Love the Lord with all your heart," the man said. "And love your neighbor as yourself."

"Right," Jesus said. "Sell everything you own. Come and follow Me."

The man was sad. He would not do this. Jesus was sad, too.

✚ Pray

Dear Jesus, please be the most important thing in my life.

> But more than anything else,
> put God's work first.
> Matthew 6:33

Making Our Goal

1 Corinthians 9:15-27

Think

Have you ever tried to talk to someone that did not seem to understand you?

Learn

Paul loved Jesus. He told people about Jesus. That was his goal.

Paul talked to everyone. He wanted them to listen. He did not let things get in his way. He had a goal. We should tell our friends about Jesus. That should be our goal.

✝ Pray

Dear Jesus, please show me how to reach my friends for You.

> I do everything I can to win
> everyone I possibly can.
> 1 Corinthians 9:22

Obeying God

Exodus 19-20

Think

Do you like rules? Why? Why not? Why are there rules?

Learn

God told Moses to come to the top of the mountain.

God said to Moses, "I am the Lord your God. I freed you from slavery. You will be My people."

God gave Moses rules. The people would obey. They knew God wanted what was best for them.

God wants us to obey His rules, too. God will be happy. Then we will be happy, too.

 Pray

Dear Jesus, please help me obey the rules God has given me.

Direct me by your command!
I love to do what you say.
Psalm 119:35

Telling God "Thank You"

Luke 17:11-19

 **? Think**

When someone does something nice for you, what do you do?

Learn

Psalms is filled with songs to God. It was the first hymn book. Many psalms say "thank you" to God.

God likes it when we thank Him. Then He knows that we like what He did.

Jesus helped many people. Most people thanked Him. One time Jesus healed ten sick people. Only one thanked Him. This made Jesus sad.

 **Pray**

Dear Jesus, thank You for all You have done for me.

> Our God, we thank you for being
> so near to us! Everyone celebrates
> your wonderful deeds.
>
> Psalm 75:1

Telling God We Are Sorry

John 18:15-27; 21:15-19

Think

How do you feel when you've done something wrong?
What makes you feel better?

Learn

Peter was sad. He had let Jesus down. Peter had lied. He had said he did not know Jesus.

Soon Peter saw Jesus. He said he was sorry. He asked Jesus to forgive Him. Jesus did.

Jesus will forgive us, too. We have to tell Him we are sorry.

✚ Pray

Dear Jesus, please forgive me for the wrong things I do.

> But if we confess our sins to God,
> he can always be trusted to forgive
> us and take our sins away.
>
> 1 John 1:9

Waiting for God

Exodus 3, 14

? Think

How do you feel when you have to wait for something?

Learn

The Israelites were slaves. They asked God to save them. God told them to wait. Then He sent Moses to save them.

Moses led the people out of Egypt. They had to wait, but God saved them.

God has plans for us. We may have to wait to see what they are.

✝ Pray

Dear Jesus, help me to trust You even when I have to wait.

Be brave and strong and trust the LORD.
Psalm 27:14

Worshiping God Alone

Exodus 19; John 6:15

Think

When was the last time you wanted to be alone?
What did you do?

Learn

Jesus spent time alone with God. Moses spent time alone with God. This pleased God.

Jesus prayed. And God told Jesus what to do.

Moses listened to God also. Then Moses knew what to tell the people.

We can spend time alone with God, too. We can tell God that we love Him.

✝ Pray

Dear God, please help me listen when You speak to my heart.

Pray to your Father in private.
Matthew 6:6

Encouraging Others

Acts 4:36; 12:25-13:3

Think

How do you make your friends feel when you're with them?

Learn

Paul had friends to encourage him. This helped Paul. It kept him going.

It is easy to be discouraged. We need friends to encourage us. We want to encourage our friends. This helps them want to do the right thing. This pleases God.

 **Pray**

Dear Jesus, please teach me how to encourage my friends.

Encourage and help each other.
1 Thessalonians 5:11

Forgiving and Forgetting

Matthew 18:21-35

 **Think**

When was the last time someone did something wrong to you?

 **Learn**

A man owed a lot of money. The man he owed did not make him pay. He was forgiven. The man who was forgiven was owed a small amount. He made the one who owed him pay.

The first man was not fair. He was treated well. He should treat others well, too.

God forgives us for what we do. We should forgive and forget.

 **Pray**

Dear Jesus, please help me forgive my friends.

If you forgive others for the
wrongs they do to you, your Father
in heaven will forgive you.

Matthew 6:14

Giving Up Our Rights

Philippians 2:6-11

Think

When was a time someone tried to take advantage of you? What did you do?

Learn

Jesus always obeyed God. He even gave up His own rights in order to obey.

Jesus was dying on the cross. Some soldiers made fun of Him. What did Jesus do? He did not try to get even. He asked God to forgive them.

We should obey God, too. It may mean giving up our own rights. This is a small price to pay to obey God.

 **Pray**

Dear Jesus, please show me how to act when people are mean to me.

> But I tell you to love your enemies
> and pray for anyone who mistreats you.
> Matthew 5:44

Helping Others

Acts 9:1-19

 **Think**

Have you ever helped someone who was not nice to you?

 **Learn**

Before Paul loved Jesus, he was mean.

Jesus asked Paul for help. Then Paul loved Jesus, too. He was not mean.

God told a man to help Paul. The man was scared of Paul. He knew Paul had been mean.

God says we should help everyone. Even someone who has been mean.

✝ Pray

Dear Jesus, I want to help people this week. Please show me how.

Use your [freedom] as an opportunity
to serve each other with love.
Galatians 5:13

Helping Others Live

2 Timothy 3:1-17

Think

Have you ever tried to tell someone they are doing something wrong?

Learn

The Bible is God's Word. God uses it to show people when they are doing wrong things.

Timothy had to tell people they were doing wrong things. He used the Bible to do this.

Paul said the Bible helps people stop doing wrong things. It helps them know the right thing.

The Bible helps us, too. It shows us how to do the right thing.

 **Pray**

Dear Jesus, how can I help someone do the right thing?

Understanding your word gives light
to the minds of ordinary people.
Psalm 119:130

Looking Out for Others

John 6:1-14; Philippians 2:1-4

Think

How do you try to help your friends? Do you help them even if it is hard for you?

Learn

Jesus cared about others. Many people came to hear Him. Jesus gave them all food. He showed He cared.

We should care, too. Jesus wants us all to get along. We should not just think of ourselves. We should be like Jesus.

What would happen if we all did that? The world would be better. Right?

✝ Pray

Dear Jesus, please help me think of others before I think of myself.

Care about them as much
as you care about yourselves.
Philippians 2:4

Loyalty to the End

Genesis 1; Exodus 4; 1 Samuel 20; John 15:13-15; Acts 4-6

? Think

Who are some of your closest friends? Would they be loyal to you no matter what?

Learn

God wants us to have friends. God is happy when we are good friends to others.

The Bible tells us about many good friends. They helped each other. This made God happy.

The best friend of all is Jesus. He gave His life for us. He will do anything for us. We should try to be that kind of friend, too.

 Pray

Dear Jesus, please make me a better friend to someone today.

> A true friend is closer
> than your own family.
> Proverbs 18:24

Picking Friends

Genesis 37

? Think

How did you choose your friends? When did any of your
friends make you do something for which you were sorry?

 ## Learn

We read about many friends in the Bible. These friends
helped each other. They helped each other do the right thing.

Bad friends get us in trouble. Joseph's brothers were
not good friends. The brothers were mean to Joseph. They
helped each other do the wrong thing.

We must choose good friends. Good friends help us do the
right thing.

✝ Pray

Dear Jesus, please give me good friends who help me obey You.

Wise friends make you wise.
Proverbs 13:20

Sacrificing for Others

Luke 10:25-37

? Think

When was the last time you gave up something to help a friend?

 Learn

Jesus gave us two laws. First, love the Lord. Second, love your neighbor.

Giving up your life is real love. Jesus did that. He gave up His life for us.

Jesus told about a good man. He saw a hurt man by the road. He helped the man. This is called sacrifice. Sacrifice is giving to help others. Sacrifice is part of love. It makes Jesus happy.

Pray

Dear Jesus, please show me what I can sacrifice to help someone.

> Children, you show love for others by truly helping them.
>
> 1 John 3:18

Serving Others

John 13:1-20

 **Think**

When was the last time you helped someone? What did you do?

What is the best way you can help others?

Learn

Many people do not like to serve others. But Jesus taught us to serve.

Jesus washed dirty feet. He served others. He taught us to serve.

We all have "gifts." These are things we are good at. We are to use our "gifts." We use them to serve others.

- 144 -

Pray

Dear Jesus, please help me to use my gifts to serve others.

If you want to be great, you must
be the servant of all the others.
Matthew 20:26

Sharing with Others

Acts 2:40-47

Think

How do you feel when one of your friends is sad?
What do you do?

Learn

The early Christians liked to be together. They shared with each other. They gave things to each other. They shared the good times. They also shared the bad times.

Peter and John were in jail. This was a bad time. All the people were sad. Soon they were set free. Then people were happy.

We can share with others, too. We can share with people in our church.

✝ Pray

Dear Jesus, please let me share something important with a friend.

When others are happy, be happy with them, and when they are sad, be sad.

Romans 12:15

Being Kind to Everyone

Matthew 5:38-42; Romans 12:9-21

Think

What do you do when people are mean to you?

Learn

We should be kind to everyone. Some people are not kind to us. We should even be kind to them.

Some people are not this way. They try to pay others back. Jesus does not like this. He does not want us to act this way. He wants us to obey Him.

If we obey, we are acting like Jesus. This makes Jesus happy.

✝ Pray

Dear Jesus, please help me be kind to those who are mean to me.

If your enemies are hungry,
give them something to eat.
Proverbs 25:21-22

Praying for Those Who Do Mean Things

Matthew 5:43-48

? Think

Have you ever helped someone who was mean to you? What did you do? Why?

 Learn

Life was hard for the first Christians. Some people hated Jesus. They were mean.

Jesus told the Christians what to do. He said, "Be kind to your enemies. Pray for those who are mean to you."

It worked. They prayed for their enemies. Then they did not act so mean. God helped the Christians to be nicer, too. We should do this, too.

✚ Pray

Dear Jesus, when people are mean, help me to pray for them.

Pray for those who spitefully
use you and persecute you.
Matthew 5:44

Avoiding Bad Situations

Genesis 39

? Think

When have you had trouble doing the right thing? Why was it hard?

Learn

Sometimes it is hard to do the right thing. Joseph loved God. One day it was hard for him to obey God. What could Joseph do?

Joseph ran away. Then he could obey God.

Sometimes it is hard for us to obey God. But we can do what Joseph did. Run away!

✚ Pray

Dear Jesus, please keep me from places where I might do wrong.

> Respect the LORD
> and stay away from evil.
> Proverbs 3:7

Resisting Temptation

Genesis 39; Psalm 139-144; Matthew 4

 **Think**

When was the last time you thought about doing something wrong? Did you do it? Why? Why not?

 **Learn**

How can we keep from doing the wrong thing?

When Joseph was tempted, he ran away. Sometimes that is best. We can play with other friends. David was tempted to do wrong. He prayed.

When Jesus was tempted to do wrong, He quoted from the Bible.

God wants us to obey Him. We may need help to do the right thing. God will help if we ask Him.

✝ Pray

Dear Jesus, please help me when I am tempted to do wrong.

God will show you how to
escape from your temptations.
1 Corinthians 10:13

Using the Bible to Win

Luke 4:1-11

 **Think**

How do you know the right thing to do? Is it easy to always know what is right?

 **Learn**

Jesus was in the desert. He was tempted to do wrong. He used God's Word. It helped Him do the right thing. The Bible is God's Word. The Bible will help us do the right thing. It can help us obey God.

Everyone is tempted to do wrong. We can use the Bible to win.

✝ Pray

Dear Jesus, please let the Bible guide me to obey You.

By your teachings, LORD, I am warned;
by obeying them, I am greatly rewarded.
Psalm 19:11

Believing the Impossible

Exodus 5-14; Mark 9:1-29

 **Think**

What can you think of that would never happen?

 **Learn**

God does many things. Some do not seem possible. Once His people were trapped. They had to cross a sea. God split the water. His people were saved. It was a miracle.

Jesus did miracles, too. He healed the sick. He walked on water. God helped Jesus. God can help us, too. There is nothing God cannot do.

✝ **Pray**

Dear Jesus, I am thankful You can do miracles.

> *God can do anything.*
> Mark 10:27

Trusting God When We are Scared

Luke 8:22-25; Acts 16:16-34

Think

When was the last time you were scared?
What did you do?

Learn

The disciples were scared during a storm. They asked Jesus for help. Jesus stopped the storm.

Paul and Silas were in jail. They were scared. They sang songs to God. They had learned to trust in God.

Jesus' friends learned to trust Him. He would take care of them. God will take care of us, too.

✝ Pray

Dear Jesus, when I am scared, please remind me to pray to You.

God is our mighty fortress, always
ready to help in times of trouble.

Psalm 46:1

Willing to Help Others

Luke 2:1-20

 **Think**

When was the last time you helped someone?
How did you help?
Do you like to help others?

 **Learn**

We need help. We need to be saved. God's Son, Jesus, can help us. He can be our Savior.

Jesus had to leave heaven. When Jesus left heaven, He left His glory as God's Son. He had to be a servant. Jesus came to earth to help us. He came to save us. We can be like Jesus and help others.

✝ Pray

Dear Jesus, thank You for helping me. Let me help others too.

He gave up everything and became a
slave, when he became like one of us.
Philippians 2:7

Living for God

Luke 2:21-38

Think

What would you like to do when you grow up? Why?
What would you like to do with your life?

Learn

Jesus was a baby. His mom and dad wanted to please God. So they did what God told them to do. They took baby Jesus to the temple. They knew Jesus would want to please God too. They knew God loved Jesus.

Simeon saw Jesus. He told Mary that her child would save the world.

Your life can be special if you can live your life for God.

 Pray

Dear Jesus, help me to live my life for You.

If I live, it will be for Christ.
Philippians 1:21

Thinking About God

Luke 2:41-50

 **Think**

What do you like to think about most? Why?
What do you try not to think about? Why?

 **Learn**

One day Jesus and His mom and dad took a trip. They went to Jerusalem. They stayed a few days. Then it was time to go home. But Jesus' mom and dad could not find Him. They were worried. They looked and looked.

Jesus was in God's house, the temple. He was talking about God with the people there.

Jesus liked to think about God. Do you?

 **Pray**

Dear God, please help me to think about You more this week.

Think about what is up there,
not about what is here on earth.
Colossians 3:2

Obeying Your Parents

Luke 2:51

Think

Do you always obey your mom and dad? Why? Why not?

Learn

Jesus grew up in Nazareth. Mary was His mom, and Joseph was His dad. Joseph was a carpenter.

Jesus knows all things. So Jesus knew more than His mom and dad! But He still obeyed them.

Jesus made God happy when He obeyed His mom and dad. Obey your mom and dad. You will make God happy too.

 Pray

Dear Jesus, please help me to obey my mom and dad better.

Children, you belong to the Lord,
and you do the right thing when
you obey your parents.
Ephesians 6:1

Growing Up

Luke 2:52

Think

Are you getting taller? Are you learning how to play with friends? Are you learning more about God?

Learn

Jesus grew up in Nazareth. He made friends. And He learned how to play with His friends. Jesus grew closer to God too. He went to the temple every week. And He read the Scriptures.

Growing taller is only one way to grow. Jesus grew in other ways too. How are you growing?

✝ Pray

Dear Jesus, help me to grow up in every way.

Jesus became wise, and his
body grew strong. God was pleased
with him and so were the people.

Luke 2:52

Obedience to God

Matthew 3:13-17

? Think

Do you obey your mom and dad? How do they feel when you do not obey them? Do you obey God? How do you think God feels when you do not obey Him?

 Learn

John the Baptist told people to tell God they were sorry for not obeying God. He baptized people who did.

Jesus went to see John. He wanted John to baptize Him too. He had not sinned. But Jesus wanted to obey God.

So John baptized Him. And God said, "This is my own dear Son, and I am pleased with Him."

Pray

Dear Jesus, help me to obey. Teach me how to do the right thing.

> Christ was humble. He obeyed
> God and even died on a cross.
> Philippians 2:8

Trusting in the Bible

Luke 4:1-13

? Think

Have you ever been told to do a thing that is wrong? What did you do?
What is the best way to keep yourself from doing the wrong thing?

 Learn

Jesus was told to do the wrong thing too. Satan wanted Jesus to disobey God. What do you think Jesus did? He quoted the Scripture to Satan! When we use the Bible, we use God's Word. Nothing is as strong as that!

Your friends may tell you to do the wrong thing. Think of a Bible verse. God will help you do the right thing.

✝ Pray

Dear Jesus, please help me to obey You all the time.

So put on all the armor that God
gives . . . you will still be standing firm.
Ephesians 6:13

Being Concerned About Everything

John 2:1-12

 **Think**

Do you help your friends when they need help with things? Even if the things do not seem important?

 **Learn**

Jesus went to a wedding. Jesus' mom was there. So were His friends, the disciples. But there was a problem. There was no drink left. Jesus' mom asked Him to help.

Jesus helped. He turned plain water into the best drink. We should help our friends too.

✝ Pray

Dear Jesus, I want to help people just like You did.

Our people should learn to
spend their time doing something
useful and worthwhile.
Titus 3:14

Loving the Church

John 2:13-22

? Think

What is your favorite place to go? Why? What do you like to do there?

 Learn

Jesus liked to go to God's house. But one time He was not happy there. People were selling things. That was not right. God's house is for prayer and worship.

Jesus was mad. He made a whip. Then He swung the whip. He knocked over the tables. The people selling things had to leave God's house.

God's house was special to Jesus.

✝ Pray

Dear Jesus, thank You for giving me a special house where I can learn about You.

It made me glad to hear them say,
"Let's go to the house of the LORD!"

Psalm 122:1

Accepting Everyone

John 3:1-21

? Think

Is there a person you do not like? Who? Why do you not like that person? Would you help that person if he or she came to you for help?

Learn

Nicodemus was a Pharisee. Pharisees did not like Jesus. One night Nicodemus came to see Jesus. He had some things to ask Jesus. He made sure no one saw him. He did not want his friends to know he went to see Jesus.

Jesus was not mean to Nicodemus. He told him more about God.

Do you know someone who is mean to you? What would you do if he or she came to you for help?

✝ **Pray**

Dear Jesus, I want to be like You. I want to help people, even ones who are mean to me.

Love your enemies and pray
for anyone who mistreats you.
Matthew 5:44

Being Friendly to Everyone

John 4:1-26

 **Think**

Are you friends with everyone? Do you talk with everyone? Why? Why not?

 **Learn**

Jesus was tired. He sat down to rest. Soon a woman came. She wanted to get a drink from the well. Jesus asked her for a drink too. She was shocked that He spoke to her. Jesus was a Jew. She was a Samaritan. Jews did not speak to Samaritans. But Jesus was nice to all people.

Do you love all people? Is everyone your friend? Jesus loved all people.

✝ Pray

Dear Jesus, help me to be friendly to everyone, not just my friends.

A friend is always a friend.
Proverbs 17:17

Knowing God's Word

Luke 4:16-30

? Think

What do you know the most about? How did you learn it? How does knowing it help you?

 Learn

Nazareth was Jesus' hometown. He grew up there. Then He went back as an adult. One day He went to worship God. Someone gave Him the Scripture to read. Jesus read it in the service. Then He told everyone what it meant.

Do you know the Scripture? Could you explain it like Jesus did?

✝ Pray

Dear Jesus, teach me God's Word. I want to be able to tell others about it, just like You did.

Open my mind and let me discover
the wonders of your Law.
Psalm 119:18

Following God

Luke 5:1-9

? Think

Do you do what you are told to do? What if someone you trusted told you to do something that made no sense?

 Learn

Simon had fished all night. But he caught no fish. Jesus got into Simon's boat. "Row the boat out into the deep water," Jesus said. "Let your nets down to catch some fish."

It did not make sense to Simon. But he did what Jesus said. And he caught many fish.

Simon was glad he did what Jesus told him. One day God may tell you to do something that does not make sense. If He does, think of Simon and his fish.

Pray

Dear Jesus, help me to obey You, even when I do not know why. I know that You will make it clear to me.

> And if they obey they will be
> successful and happy from then on.
> Job 36:11

Giving Up Things for Jesus

Luke 5:10-11

 **Think**

Have you ever had to give up one thing to get something else you wanted more? What was it? Was it worth it?

 **Learn**

Simon loved to fish. Then he met Jesus. Jesus helped him catch a lot of fish.

Jesus wanted to help Simon fish for people. He wanted Simon to tell others about Jesus. So Simon followed Jesus. He gave up a thing he loved. But he got something better. He got Jesus.

Pray

Dear Jesus, I want to follow You, too. Help me give up those things that get in the way.

If you want to save your life, you will destroy it. But if you give up your life for me, you will find it.

Matthew 16:25

Pleasing God

Mark 1:40-45

Think

Do you want to be popular? Is it the most important thing to you? Would you ever give up being popular? Why? Why not?

Learn

One day a man came to see Jesus. He was sick. He knew Jesus could help him. And Jesus did! The man was healed. He was happy. He told all his friends that Jesus made him well.

Everyone wanted to see Jesus. Jesus was very popular. But Jesus did not want to be popular. So He left town. He just wanted to please God. That was better than being popular.

✝ Pray

Dear Jesus, teach me that there are better things than being popular.

> But more than anything else, put
> God's work first and do what he wants.
>
> Matthew 6:33

Caring for People

Mark 2:1-12

Think

Have you ever had a friend break one of your toys?
Which did you care about more - your friend or your toy?

Learn

One day many people went to a house to hear Jesus talk. They filled the whole house. A man who could not walk wanted to see Jesus too. He knew Jesus could make him well. But he could not get into the house. So his friends made a hole in the roof. Then they lowered the man down to Jesus.

Jesus was not angry that they made a hole in the roof. Jesus cared more about the man than about the house.

Dear Jesus, help me to love people like You do.

Then you will live a life that
honors the Lord, and you will always
please him by doing good deeds.
Colossians 1:10

Loving the
Unlovely

Matthew 9:9-13

 **Think**

Do you know some kids who do not have many friends? Do *you* like them? Why? Why not?

 **Learn**

Matthew collected taxes. He would often take more money than he should. He did not have many friends. Not many people wanted to talk to him.

But Jesus asked Matthew to follow Him. Matthew had a party for Jesus. It was at his house. That made some people mad. They did not think Jesus should go to Matthew's house. Jesus loved Matthew and wanted to be his friend.

✝ Pray

Dear Jesus, help me to love people that even my friends do not like.

> But don't forget to help others and to share your possessions with them. This too is like offering a sacrifice that pleases God.
>
> Hebrews 13:16

Helping Others First

Luke 6:6-11

? Think

Do you like to help people? Why? Would you give up something you wanted to help them? Would you give up something you like to do to help a person? Why?

 Learn

It was the Lord's Day. Jesus saw a man with a hurt hand. The man wanted Jesus to make him well. The Jewish leaders did not think it was right to make someone well on the Lord's Day.

"Stretch out your hand," Jesus said to the man. The man stretched out his hand. Then Jesus made it well.

The Jewish leaders were mad at Jesus. But Jesus wanted to help the man. That was the right thing to do.

✚ **Pray**

Dear Jesus, bring someone into my life today who I can help.

It is right to do good on the Sabbath.
Matthew 12:12

Asking for Help

Luke 6:12-16

Think

When was the last time you were worried or scared?
What did you do?

Learn

Jesus had to choose some close friends. The friends would be with Jesus for a long time. He would teach them many things. They would tell many people about Jesus.

Jesus prayed *all night*! He asked God to help Him choose the right friends.

God helped Jesus choose the right friends. When you have a hard job to do, do what Jesus did. Pray and ask God to help you. He will.

 **Pray**

Dear Jesus, help me to pray to God each night.

Everyone who asks will receive, everyone who searches will find, and the door will be opened for everyone who knocks.

Luke 11:10

Acting on Faith

Luke 7:1-10

? Think

Would you believe one of your friends if he or she told you something would happen? Why? Why not?

Learn

A soldier had a servant who was sick. The soldier had heard about Jesus. He asked Jesus to make his servant well. Jesus started to go to the man's house.

But the man sent Jesus a message by some friends: "Just say the word, and my servant will get well."

The soldier believed in Jesus. He knew Jesus could heal his servant. All Jesus had to do was speak.

✝ Pray

Dear Jesus, help me to know that You will take care of me.

Faith that doesn't lead us to
do good deeds is all alone and dead!
James 2:17

Helping Those Who Hurt

Luke 7:11-17

 **Think**

When was the last time you felt sorry for someone?
What did you do to help?

Learn

One day Jesus saw a woman leaving a city. The woman was crying. Her son had just died. The woman's husband was already dead. The woman was all alone.

Jesus looked at the woman. He felt sorry for her. "Don't cry!" Jesus said to her.

"Get up!" Jesus said to the dead boy. The boy sat up. He was alive! The woman did not cry anymore. Jesus made her happy again.

Pray

Dear Jesus, help me to care for people like You do.

Children, you show love for
others by truly helping them, and
not merely by talking about it.
1 John 3:18

Accepting People Who Aren't Perfect

Luke 7:36-50

 **Think**

Do you know someone who is "different" from other kids?
Do your friends play with that person? Why? Why not?
Do you play with him or her? Why? Why not?

 **Learn**

Jesus went to eat at a friend's house. A woman came to see Him there. The woman had done wrong things. But she loved Jesus. She wanted Jesus to forgive her.

Jesus' friends did not think He should talk to her. They did not think she was a good person. But Jesus loved her. And Jesus forgave her. Jesus loves everyone.

 Pray

Dear Jesus, help me to love everyone.

Love comes from God, and when
we love each other, it shows that
we have been given new life.
1 John 4:7

Being Part of God's Family

Luke 8:19-21

Think

What do you like most about being in your family? Why?
What special things happen because you are in your family?

Learn

One day Jesus was teaching people about God. Jesus' mother
and brothers went to see Jesus. But there were many people.
They could not see Jesus. So they sent Him a message. "Your
mother and brothers are standing outside," the message said.

   But Jesus did not go out to see them. He said, "My mother
and my brothers are those people who hear and obey God's
message." That is us. We are part of Jesus' family!

 Pray

Dear Jesus, thank You for making me a part of Your family.

He loves us so much that he lets us
be called his children, as we truly are.
1 John 3:1

Being Alone

Matthew 8:18, 24

 **Think**

Are you always busy doing things?
Are you ever too busy?
What do you do when you have too much to do?

 **Learn**

Jesus taught people about God. He made sick people well.
Soon many people were going to see Jesus. But Jesus had to
rest. He had to be alone.

So Jesus left the crowds. He went to the other side of the
lake. He was so tired He slept in the boat.

When things get too busy for you, take time to get away.

 **Pray**

Dear Jesus, help me to know when to slow down.

> But those who trust the LORD
> will find new strength.
> Isaiah 40:31

Trusting God

Mark 4:35-41

 **Think**

When was the last time you were worried about something? What did you do? Did you trust God to take care of your problem? Why? Why not?

Learn

Jesus was tired. He told His friends, the disciples, to get in the boat. They were all going to the other side of the lake. Soon Jesus was asleep.

A storm came on the lake. Then water came in the boat. But Jesus still slept. The disciples called to Jesus for help. He woke up, Jesus told the wind to stop blowing. The storm stopped. Jesus took care of their problems. All they had to do was trust Him.

Pray

Dear Jesus, help me to come to You first when I have problems.

You, LORD God, are my protector.
Psalm 7:1

Believing in God

Luke 8:40-42, 49-56

 **Think**

Who do you turn to when you need help? Are you sure you would get help? Why? Has this person ever let you down?

Learn

Jairus had one daughter. She was 12 years old. And she was dying. Jairus begged Jesus to come to his house. He knew Jesus could help his daughter.

Then a messenger came from Jairus's house. "Your daughter has died!" the person said. Jesus told Jairus, "Don't worry! Have faith, and your daughter will get well."

Jesus went to Jairus's house. "Child, get up!" Jesus told her. The girl sat up. Jairus believed that Jesus could help his daughter. And He did.

✝ Pray

Dear Jesus, please help me to trust You more.

The prayer of an innocent person is
powerful, and it can help a lot.
James 5:16

Accepting Rejection

Luke 9:1-6

Think

When did someone not want to play with you or be your friend? How did you feel? What did you do?

Learn

The disciples saw Jesus teach about God. Now it was their turn. Jesus sent them out to the towns. They were going to tell people about God too.

"If people won't welcome you," Jesus told them, "leave the town." Some people would not like the disciples, Jesus did not want the disciples to be sad when people did not like them. Even Jesus was not liked by everyone.

Pray

Dear Jesus, help me to act like You want me to act.

God blesses those people who are treated badly for doing right. They belong to the kingdom of heaven.

Matthew 5:10

Leaning on God

Mark 6:30-44

Think

Do you try to solve problems by yourself? Or do you let someone else help you?

Learn

People came to see Jesus. Soon there were 5,000 men and many women and children. The people became hungry. But the only food was one boy's lunch of five loaves of bread and two fish.

Jesus took the food. Then He blessed it. The food fed all the people. There was even some left over! Jesus trusted in God. God took care of all those people.

✝ Pray

Dear Jesus, help me to know You will always take care of me.

With all your heart you must trust
the LORD and not your own judgement.
Proverbs 3:5

Acting on Faith

Matthew 14:22-33

Think

When your mom or dad picks you up, are you worried? Why? Why not?
Would you let someone you did not know pick you up? Why?

Learn

The disciples were in a boat. They saw a man walking on the water. They thought it was a ghost. But it was Jesus.

So Peter got out of the boat. He walked on the water too. Then Peter got scared. And he started to sink.

Jesus pulled Peter out of the water. When Peter had faith in Jesus, he could walk on the water.

 **Pray**

Dear Jesus, help me to keep my eyes on You.

God can do anything.
Matthew 19:26

Being Clean on the Inside

Matthew 15:1-20

Think

Do you wash your hands before you eat? Why? How do you wash the inside of your heart?

Learn

The Jewish leaders were mad. Jesus' disciples did not wash their hands when they ate. The Jews asked Jesus why His disciples did not follow this rule.

Jesus told them that what you eat does not make you clean or unclean. It is bad words you say that make you unclean. Your inside is what hurts you.

✝ Pray

Dear Jesus, thank You for washing me on the inside. Help me to do the right things.

These commands are nearby
and you know them by heart.
All you have to do is obey!

Deuteronomy 30:14

Sharing Glory with Others

Matthew 17:1-13

Think

When was the last time you received credit for something you did? Did you share that credit with others? Why? Why not?

Learn

Jesus did not have to share His glory, but He did.

One day Jesus took Peter, James, and John with Him to a high mountain. Soon Jesus' clothes became white. His face started to shine like the sun. Then a bright cloud appeared.

A voice came out of the cloud. "This is my own dear Son, and I am pleased with Him. Listen to what he says!" the voice said.

Jesus wanted His friends to see that.

 **Pray**

Dear Jesus, thank You for sharing Your glory with me.

> Love each other as brothers
> and sisters and honor others
> more than you do yourself.
> Romans 12:10

Serving Others

Mark 9:33-37

 **? Think**

When have you argued with your friends about who is best?
Who won? Is there a right way to become the best?

Learn

One day the disciples took a walk. They had an argument.
Each one wanted to be great. Each one wanted to be the best.
"What were you arguing about?" Jesus asked them. They did
not tell Him.

 He sat down with them, He told them that to be great, they
must serve others.

 **Pray**

Dear Jesus, give me a time today to serve someone else.

> If you want the place of honor, you
> must become a slave and serve others!
> Mark 9:35

Having Good Friends

Matthew 18:21-35

Think

When was the last time someone asked you to forgive him or her? What did you say? Do you get tired of forgiving your friends?

Learn

"How many times should I forgive someone?" Peter asked Jesus. Jesus told him a story.

A man owed the king a lot of money. He asked the king for forgiveness. The king forgave the man. The man was happy.

Then he saw a friend. "Pay me what you owe!" he said.

The man's friend asked for forgiveness. But the man would not forgive him. Jesus told Peter that we are to forgive others with all our hearts.

✝ Pray

Dear Jesus, thank You for forgiving me. Help me to forgive my friends too.

If you forgive others for the wrongs they do to you, your Father in heaven will forgive you.

Matthew 6:14

Deciding Who Is Important

John 6:60-69

 **Think**

What was the last thing you did that was hard?
Why did you do it? Was it worth it? Why? Why not?

 **Learn**

People wanted to be with Jesus. But it was not easy. Jesus said some hard things. Many times people did not know what He meant.

Soon people started leaving Jesus. It was too hard to stay. Jesus turned to the disciples and asked if they wanted to leave Him too.

"There is no one else that we can go to!" Peter said. "Your words give eternal life."

✝ Pray

Dear Jesus, I want to follow You. Help me to know what it means to be Your friend.

> If any of you want to be my followers, you must forget about yourself. You must take up your cross and follow me.
>
> Matthew 16:24

Forgiving,
Not Punishing

John 8:1-11

? Think

When was the last time you did something wrong? Were you punished?
Were you ever not punished when you did something wrong? How did you feel?

Learn

Some men brought a woman to Jesus. They said that she did a bad thing. Jesus stooped down as if He did not hear them. He wrote in the dirt.

Jesus stood up. "If any of you have never sinned, then go ahead and throw the first stone at her!" He said. The men left. They had all done wrong. Jesus did not punish the woman. He forgave her.

✝ Pray

Dear Jesus, thank You for forgiving me when I do wrong.

Sin pays off with death. But
God's gift is eternal life given
by Jesus Christ our Lord.

Romans 6:23

Giving Glory to God

John 9:1-34

 **Think**

Have you ever had a friend who said he or she did something you did? What happened? How did it make you feel?

Learn

One day Jesus saw a blind man. Jesus spat on the ground. Then He put the mud on the man's eyes.

"Go and wash off the mud," Jesus told him.

The man obeyed. Soon he came back. He could see some people did not believe Jesus helped the man see.

But the man said, "I used to be blind, but now I can see!" He knew God had made him see.

- 232 -

✝ **Pray**

Dear Jesus, You are so great. I want people to know all You do for me.

We will always praise your glorious name. Let your glory be seen everywhere on earth.

Psalm 72:19

Taking Care of Others

John 10:1-21

 Think

When was the last time you helped a friend?
What did you do?
How does Jesus help you?

Learn

Shepherds take care of sheep. They keep sheep safe.
Shepherds make sure the sheep are fed. Sheep will die
without shepherds.

Jesus is our shepherd. He keeps us safe. He feeds us and
watches over us. The shepherd helps the sheep. Jesus helps
us.

We can make sure our friends are all right. If they need
help, we can help them. We can be like Jesus.

✝ Pray

Dear Jesus, thank You for being the Good Shepherd. Show me how I can help others.

> Since God loved us this much,
> we must love each other.
> John 4:11

Letting Others in on the Fun

Luke 10:1-24

 **Think**

When was the last time you did something good for someone else? What were you doing? How did it make you feel?

Learn

Jesus picked 72 friends. He had a big job for them to do. They would take His words to many towns.

They could heal those who were sick. And they could tell people about Jesus. Jesus let His friends do what He did. He did not want to be the only one doing good. He wanted His friends to help people too.

 **Pray**

Dear Jesus, help me to share good things with my friends.

> Instruct them to do as many good
> deeds as they can and to help everyone.
> I Timothy 6:18

Helping Our Enemies

Luke 10:25-37

 **Think**

Who was the last person you helped? What did you do?
Have you ever helped someone who was not your friend?
Why? Why not?

 **Learn**

One day Jesus told a story. Robbers beat up a Jewish man.
Then they took his money. They left the man on the side of
the road.

   Two people walked by the man. But they did not help him.
Samaritans did not like Jews. But a Samaritan stopped when
he saw the man. He helped the Jewish man feel better.

   This is how we should act. We should even help people we do
not like.

✝ Pray

Dear Jesus, I want to be more like the good Samaritan. And I want to be more like You.

Love your enemies, and be good
to everyone who hates you.

Luke 6:27

Making Jesus #1

Luke 10:38-42

 ? Think

Have you ever had more than two things to do at the same time? What did you do? How did you decide what to do?

Learn

Mary and Martha were sisters. They loved Jesus. One day Jesus ate at their house. Martha worked hard to fix a good meal. But Mary sat. She wanted to hear Jesus.

Martha was mad. "Tell her to come and help me!" she said.

"Mary has chosen what is best," Jesus said. She chose Jesus.

Jesus is the best. When we choose Him, we have done the right thing.

✝ Pray

Dear Jesus, I choose You. I want You to be the most important thing in my life.

> Love the Lord your God with all your heart, soul, and mind.
>
> Matthew 22:37

Asking God First

Luke 11:1-13

Think

When you need help, who do you ask? Why?

Learn

Jesus' friends, the disciples, wanted Jesus to teach them how to pray. So Jesus told them a story.

A man went to his friend's house at midnight. He woke him up. Then he asked him for some bread.

"Don't bother me!" his friend said. But the man kept knocking. So his friend got up and gave him what he wanted.

Jesus told them to keep praying. God wants to give you good things. He will answer your prayers if you keep asking Him.

✚ Pray

Dear Jesus, thank You for always giving me what I need.

I tell you to ask and you will receive,
search and you will find, knock and
the door will be opened for you.

Luke 11:9

Deciding Who to Follow

Luke 11:14-23

Think

When was the last time you played a game with teams?
Whose team were you on? Could you have been on both sides?
Why not?

Learn

Jesus did great things. He helped a lot of people. And He
healed many people. But some people did not believe in Jesus.
They did not know He was the Son of God.

   You cannot be for God and also against Him. Which side are
you on?

✝ Pray

Dear Jesus, I want to be on Your side. Help me to grow more like You.

> If you are not on my side,
> you are against me.
>
> Luke 11:23

Trusting God

Luke 12:13-34

Think

When was the last time you worried?
What did you worry about? Did worrying help?

Learn

One day Jesus told a story about a rich man. He had no room for all his things. So he built a bigger place to keep all his things. Then he was happy.

But God said to him, "You fool! Tonight you will die. Then who will get what you have stored up?"

Jesus did not worry about collecting things on earth. He taught others about God. We should learn about Jesus, not worry about things.

✝ Pray

Dear Jesus, I do not want to worry about things. I want to think about You.

I tell you not to worry about your life. Don't worry about having something to eat, drink, or wear.

Matthew 6:25

Fearing No One

John 11:17-46

? Think

What are you afraid of? Why? Do you think God can help you with your fear?

Learn

Mary and Martha were sad. Their brother, Lazarus, was sick. They sent word to Jesus. But when He came, their brother was already dead.

Jesus said, "Your brother will live again!" Jesus went to the grave. "Come out!" Jesus said. Lazarus walked out of the grave! He was alive! There was nothing to fear. Even death could not defeat Jesus.

✝ Pray

Dear Jesus, help me not to be afraid.

Everyone who has faith in
me will live, even if they die.

John 11:25

Thanking God

Luke 17:11-19

 **Think**

What do you do when you receive a gift? Why? What do you do when God gives you something?

Learn

Jesus was on His way to Jerusalem. He stopped at a village. He saw ten lepers, people who were very sick.

They called to Jesus, "Have pity on us!"

Jesus healed them. One of them came back to Jesus. He thanked Him for making him well. "Where are the other nine?" Jesus asked.

When God helps us, we should always thank Him.

 **Pray**

Dear Jesus, thank You for all You do for me.

It is wonderful to be grateful
and to sing your praises.
Psalm 92:1

Not Giving Up on God

Luke 18:1-8

 **Think**

When was the last time you wanted something very, very much?
What did you do? What would you have done if your parents had said no?

 **Learn**

One day Jesus told this story. A widow was sad. She went to see a judge. She wanted him to help her. At first the judge would not help her. But she kept asking him.

Finally, the judge helped her. She asked him so much he was afraid she would wear him out. God will help us too. We just need to keep asking.

 **Pray**

Dear Jesus, help me to keep praying.

Never give up praying.
Colossians 4:2

Being Humble with God

Luke 18:9-14

Think

Name some of your friends who are proud of themselves. Why do they feel this way?

Learn

Jesus told a story about two men. The two men went to pray. One man thanked God that he was not like other people. The man was proud of himself. The other man said, "God, have pity on me! I am such a sinner."

Which man do you think made God happy? The second man. God is not happy when we are proud. He is happy when we are humble.

✝ Pray

Dear Jesus, help me not to be proud. Help me be humble.

If you put yourself above others,
you will be put down. But if you
humble yourself, you will be honored.
Luke 18:14

Loving Everyone

Luke 18:15-17

Think

Have you ever felt as if no one loved you? Why?

Learn

Jesus was busy. Many people came to see Him. One day parents came to see Jesus. They brought their children.

The disciples stopped them. They did not think Jesus had time to see children. But Jesus said, "Let the children come to me!"

Jesus loved all people, including children.

 **Pray**

Dear Jesus, help me to have time for everyone.

If you love each other, everyone
will know that you are my disciples.
John 13:35

Loving God Most

Luke 18:18-30

? Think

Who is your best friend? Why? What would you give up for that person? Why?

 ## Learn

A rich man spoke to Jesus one day. "What must I do to have eternal life?" he asked.

"You know the commandments," Jesus told him.

"I have obeyed all these commandments," the man said.

"There is one thing you still need to do," Jesus said. "Sell everything you own! Give the money to the poor."

The man walked away. He did not want to do that. So he gave up following Jesus.

✝ Pray

Dear Jesus, help me to always make You first in my life.

Come and be my follower.
Luke 18:22

Helping Others

Luke 19:1-10

 **Think**

When was the last time you helped someone? What did you do?
How did it make you feel?

 **Learn**

Jesus passed through Jericho one day. Many people rushed to see Him. Zacchaeus wanted to see Him too. But he had a problem. He was short.

So he ran ahead of the crowd. He climbed a big tree. Then he could see Jesus too.

Jesus saw him. He knew Zacchaeus needed help. "Hurry down!" Jesus said to him. "I want to stay with you."

Jesus went to Zacchaeus's house. He helped Zacchaeus.

 Pray

Dear Jesus, show me how I can help someone today.

> Obey God's message! Don't fool
> yourselves by just listening to it.
> James 1:22

Worshiping Jesus

John 12:1-8

 **Think**

How do you tell Jesus that you love Him? Do you go to church Sunday morning? What do you do there?

 **Learn**

One night Jesus was with Mary and Martha.

Mary took a bottle of perfume. It cost a lot of money. She poured the perfume on Jesus' feet. Then she wiped His feet with her hair!

Judas was mad. He wanted her to sell it and give the money to the poor.

"Leave her alone!" Jesus said. He knew she loved Him. That is why she did it. How do you tell Jesus that you love Him?

Pray

Dear Jesus, I love You. Help me to think about You in church.

You are worshiped by everyone!
We all sing praises to you.

Psalm 66:4

Honoring Jesus as King

Matthew 21:1-11

Think

What does a king do?
How do people act when they are near a king? Why?

Learn

Jesus entered Jerusalem. It was a special visit.

He sat on a young donkey. The people spread their coats on the ground. The donkey walked over them. Some people cut branches off the trees. They waved them at Jesus.

They all shouted, "Hooray for the Son of David! God bless the one who comes in the name of the Lord."

They were cheering for their King. Jesus is the King.

 **Pray**

Dear Jesus, You are my King. Help me to be Your loyal follower.

I will praise you, my God and
King, and always honor your name.

Psalm 145:1

Doing What God Wants

Luke 19:41-44

 **Think**

How do your parents feel when you disobey them? Why?
How do you think Jesus feels when we disobey Him?

 **Learn**

Jesus loved Jerusalem. It was God's city. Jesus wanted the
people who lived there to obey God.

Jesus went to Jerusalem for the last time. He thought of
how the people had not obeyed God. Jesus thought of how
God would punish them. Jesus was sad. He cried.

 Pray

Dear Jesus, help me not to make You sad.

Show me your paths and
teach me to follow.
Psalm 25:4

Praying and Believing

Mark 11:12-14, 20-26

? Think

When was the last time God gave you or your parents something you prayed for? When you pray for something, do you really believe God will give it to you? Why? Why not?

 Learn

Jesus and His disciples were hungry. Then they saw a fig tree. Jesus thought they could get something to eat. But the fig tree had only leaves on it. "Never again will anyone eat fruit from this tree!" Jesus said.

The next day the disciples saw the same tree. It was dried up. "Have faith in God!" Jesus said.

When we believe in God, great things can happen.

✝ Pray

Dear Jesus, I believe in You. Please help me to have more faith when I pray.

Everything you ask for in prayer
will be yours, if you only have faith.
Mark 11:24

Winning with Jesus

Mark 11:27-33

? Think

Do you know anyone who always wins? Do you know anyone who tries to trick others?

 Learn

The Jewish leaders wanted to trick Jesus. "What right do you have to do these things? Who gave you this authority?" they asked.

Jesus was too smart for them. He asked them a question. The leaders did not know how to answer. They were trapped! "We don't know," they said to Jesus.

"Then I won't tell you who gave me the right to do what I do," Jesus said. Jesus always wins. When we follow Him, we win too.

✝ Pray

Dear Jesus, thank You for letting me win with You.

Thank God for letting our Lord
Jesus Christ give us the victory!
1 Corinthians 15:57

Giving All to Jesus

Mark 12:41-44

? Think

Do you give an offering at church? Why? Would you give an offering if you did not have much money? Why? Why not?

Learn

Jesus and His disciples were talking. They stood by the temple. People came to give their offerings. One man gave a lot of money.

Then a woman came. She was poor. She gave her last few coins. "This poor widow has put in more than all the others," Jesus said. He knew she gave everything she had.

God wants us to give from our hearts.

✝ Pray

Dear Jesus, what I have, I want to give to You.

Each of you must make up your
own mind about how much to give.
2 Corinthians 9:7

Helping Jesus

Mark 14:12-16

 **Think**

What is the most special meal at your house? Thanksgiving? Christmas? Who fixes the meal? Do you help?

 **Learn**

The Passover was a special meal. Jesus wanted to eat it with His disciples. He asked some of them to help Him. They got things ready for the meal. A man gave them a room to use.

You can help Jesus too. You can give money that will help a missionary tell about Jesus. You can give food to those who are hungry. When you help others, you help Jesus.

✝ Pray

Dear Jesus, help me know what You want me to do.

> Whenever you did it for any of
> my people, no matter how unimportant
> they seemed, you did it for me.
>
> Matthew 25:40

Letting God Pay People Back

Mark 14:17-21

? Think

Have you ever had a friend act mean to you? What happened? Did you act mean back to him or her? Why?

Learn

The disciples were Jesus' friends. He taught them many things. He loved them. Jesus knew one of them would do something mean to Him. He would turn Jesus over to His enemies.

Jesus told the disciples that one of them would betray Him.

They were very sad. "Surely you don't mean me!" each one said.

Jesus did not try to get even. He left that to God.

✝ Pray

Dear Jesus, help me to trust in Your fairness.

Don't try to get even.
Let God take revenge.

Romans 12:19

Willing to Do Small Jobs

John 13:1-11

? Think

Would you do any job to help a friend? Or do you think some jobs are too small for you?

 Learn

Jesus and the disciples had walked a long way. Their feet were dirty. Often a servant washed feet. But Jesus washed the disciples' feet!

They did not understand. Jesus was the Son of God. Why should He wash their feet?

"You don't really know what I am doing," Jesus said, "but later you will understand."

Jesus was serving His friends. No job was too small for Jesus. Can any job be too small for us?

 Pray

Dear Jesus, sometimes I think I am too big for small jobs.
Help me remember that You washed dirty feet.

Anyone who can be trusted
in little matters can also be
trusted in important matters.
Luke 16:10

Forgetting Our Problems

Luke 22:14-23

 **Think**

Do you have the Lord's Supper at your church? What happens?

Why do people take the Lord's Supper? What do they think about?

 **Learn**

Jesus would have a long night. Then He would die.

Jesus had the Passover meal with His disciples first. He wanted them to remember what happened. He gave them the Lord's Supper. When they took it, Jesus told them to think about Him. Jesus forgot His problems. He thought about the disciples. When we take the Lord's Supper, we can forget our problems too. We can think about Jesus.

✝ Pray

Dear Jesus, thank You, for giving me a good way to remember You.

When you eat this bread and drink from this cup, you tell about his death until he comes.

1 Corinthians 11:26

Praying for Others

Luke 22:31-34

 **Think**

When was the last time you prayed for a friend? Why did you pray for him or her? What happened?

 **Learn**

Jesus cared for the disciples. He loved them very much. Many times the Jewish leaders did not like what the disciples did. But Jesus stood up for them.

Jesus prayed for the disciples too. That was one of the best things Jesus did for them. He prayed a lot for a disciple named Peter.

"I have prayed that your faith will be strong," Jesus told him.

Do you want to help your friends? Pray for them.

 Pray

Dear Jesus, teach me how to pray for my friends like You prayed for Your friends.

> Friends, please pray for us.
> 1 Thessalonians 5:25

Preparing Through Prayer

Luke 22:39-46

Think

When was the last time you had to do something hard? Did you worry about it? What did you do?

Learn

Jesus did not want to die. What could He do? He prayed to God.

Jesus was so upset He started sweating. The sweat dropped from Him like blood. God did something special. He sent an angel to help Jesus.

Jesus prayed. And God helped Him. God will help us, too, if we ask Him.

 Pray

Dear Jesus, sometimes I get scared when I have to do something hard. Jesus, help me to pray and ask You for help.

> Father ... do what you want,
> and not what I want.
>
> Luke 22:42

Allowing God's Will to Be Done

John 18:1-11

 **Think**

Did your parents ever tell you to do something you did not like? What was it? Did you do it?

 **Learn**

Jesus was with the disciples in the garden. Suddenly a group of men came. They had weapons. Peter took his sword. He was ready to fight. He cut an ear off one of the men.

"Put your sword away," Jesus said to Peter. He knew He must do what God wanted.

Jesus did not want them to fight. Jesus knew everything that happened to Him was part of God's plan.

✝ Pray

Dear Jesus, I want to obey You. I want to do what You want.

> You are my God. Show me what you
> want me to do, and let your gentle
> Spirit lead me in the right path.
>
> Psalm 143:10

Putting Everything in God's Hands

John 19:1-16

**Think**

When was the last time your parents solved a problem for you? Why did you let them solve it? Would you let God solve a problem for you? Why? Why not?

Learn

Jesus was brought to Pilate. Pilate was an important ruler. He told Jesus that he had the power to decide whether Jesus should die.

Jesus did not agree. He said, "If God had not given you the power, you couldn't do anything at all to Me." Pilate was not in charge. God was in charge.

✝ Pray

Dear Jesus, I want You to be in charge of my life. Your way is best.

The world and the desires it causes are disappearing. But if we obey God, we will live forever.
1 John 2:17

Taking Our Place

Matthew 27:11-26

 **Think**

Has someone else ever been punished for something you did? What happened? How did you feel?

 **Learn**

The crowd brought Jesus to Pilate. Pilate did not know what to do. He wanted to let Jesus go free. He could let someone in jail go free each year.

"Which prisoner do you want me to set free?" he asked the crowd.

"Barabbas!" they yelled. Barabbas had done many bad things. But Pilate set him free. Jesus died in his place. Jesus died in our place too.

✝ Pray

Dear Jesus, thank You for dying in my place. Thank You for taking my punishment.

> The greatest way to show love
> for friends is to die for them.
> John 15:13

Being Loving

Luke 23:26-38

? Think

Have people ever made fun of you? What did they say?
How did it make you feel? What did you do? What did you
want to do?

Learn

The crowd led Jesus out of the city. He was going to die.
Many people were crying. They were very sad.

Some soldiers made fun of Jesus. "He should save himself,"
they shouted, "if he really is God's chosen Messiah!"

Jesus just prayed for them. "Father," Jesus said, "forgive
these people! They don't know what they're doing."

Do people make fun of you? Do what Jesus did. Pray. Ask
God to forgive them.

✝ Pray

Dear Jesus, help me to pray for people who make fun of me.

But I tell you to love your enemies
and pray for anyone who mistreats you.
Matthew 5:44

Looking on the Inside

Luke 23:39-43

Think

Can you tell what someone is like by looking at him or her? Why? Why not? Have you ever been wrong about someone?

Learn

Two men died with Jesus. They had done bad things. One of them made fun of Jesus. But the other man told him to be quiet.

"Remember me when You come into power!" the man said to Jesus.

"I promise that today you will be with Me in paradise," Jesus told him.

Jesus looked past the man's outside. He saw what he was like on the inside.

Pray

Dear Jesus, help me to look past the way people are on the outside. I want to see people on the inside.

Your words show what is in your hearts.
Luke 6:45

Helping Our Parents

John 19:25-27

 **Think**

When was the last time your parents helped you?
When was the last time you helped them? How could you help them again?

 **Learn**

Jesus would die soon. His mother would be alone. Jesus saw her there at the cross.

John, one of the disciples, was there too. Jesus looked at His mother. "This man is now your son," Jesus said. Then He looked at John. "She is now your mother," He said.

That night Jesus' mother went to stay with John. Jesus never forgot His mother. Jesus took good care of her, even when He was on the cross.

✚ Pray

Dear Jesus, thank You for giving me parents who care for me. Help me to know how I can help them.

Respect your father and your mother, and you will live a long and successful life.

Deuteronomy 5:16

Keeping Our Promises

Luke 24:1-8

 **Think**

Have you ever broken a promise? Why? Do you think God breaks His promises? Why? Why not?

 **Learn**

Jesus told His friends that He would rise from the dead. But they forgot. Jesus was dead. They were sad.

In the morning some women visited the tomb. But the tomb was empty! Two angels stood next to them. "Jesus is not here! He has been raised from death," they told the women. They reminded the women of Jesus' promise to rise to life.

The women remembered. Jesus had kept His promise.

✝ Pray

Dear Jesus, thank You for keeping Your promises.

We must hold tightly to
the hope that we say is ours.
After all, we can trust the one
who made the agreement with us.
Hebrews 10:23

Letting Jesus Teach Us

Luke 24:13-32

 **? Think**

Do you know everything? If you have a question, whom do you ask? Why?

Learn

Two men were walking on the road. It was right after Jesus died. They talked about what happened. Then Jesus appeared. He walked with them. But they did not know who He was. "What were you talking about as you walked along?" Jesus asked them. They told Him what happened in Jerusalem.

   "Why can't you understand?" Jesus said. Then He explained the Scriptures to them.

✚ Pray

Dear Jesus, sometimes I have trouble understanding the Bible. Please help me know what it means.

Teach me to follow, LORD,
and lead me on the right path
because of my enemies.
Psalm 27:11

Helping Others Learn

John 20:24-31

Think

When was the last time you taught something to a friend?
What did you do? How did it make you feel? Why?

Learn

The disciples knew Jesus was alive. They had seen Him. But
one disciple, Thomas, had not seen Him and did not believe
Jesus was alive. He wanted to see the nail scars.

A week later, the disciples were together once more.
Thomas was with them. Jesus was there. Thomas saw Him.

"Stop doubting and have faith!" Jesus told Thomas. Jesus
helped Thomas learn. We can help our friends learn too.

 **Pray**

Dear Jesus, help me to teach others when they do not understand.

> Without faith no one can
> please God. We must believe that
> God is real and that he rewards
> everyone who searches for him.
>
> Hebrews 11:6

Giving Our Friends Another Chance

John 21:15-19

 Think

When was the last time a friend did something to hurt you? Did you forgive him or her? Did you trust the person again?

Learn

Peter made Jesus sad. He told people that Jesus was not his friend. Peter knew he had done a bad thing. As soon as he did it, he cried. Jesus was alive and with Peter again. Jesus did not get mad at Peter. Jesus asked Peter one thing, "Do you love me?"

Jesus had a big job for Peter. He wanted him to help others. He gave him a second chance. Peter went on to tell many people about Jesus.

✝ Pray

Dear Jesus, thank You for giving me a second chance. Help me to give my friends a second chance too.

Always be humble and gentle.
Patiently put up with each
other and love each other.
Ephesians 4:2

Sending Others to Help

Acts 1:1-8

 **Think**

Have you ever gotten help for someone? Why? Could other people help better than you could? Why?

Learn

It was time to say good-bye to Jesus. All the disciples were together. Jesus would soon leave. Then the disciples would be alone. Jesus knew they would need help.

"Wait here for the Father to give you the Holy Spirit," Jesus said. He had told them about the Holy Spirit. The Holy Spirit would help them.

![Pray] **Pray**

Father, thank You for sending the Holy Spirit. Help me to be willing to help others too.

Then I will ask the Father to send you the Holy Spirit who will help you and always be with you.

John 14:16

Telling Others About Jesus

Matthew 28:16-20

Think

Have you ever told a friend about Jesus? Why? Why not? What did you say? What happened?

Learn

Jesus taught the disciples many things. He taught them what to do. He taught them how to live.

It was time for Jesus to leave. But He had one more thing to tell them.

Jesus told them to go and make disciples. He said, "I will be with you always."

The disciples would not forget that. They would go many places. They would tell many people about Jesus. And Jesus would be with them.

Pray

Dear Jesus, thank You for always being with me. Help me to tell someone about You this week.

> Go and preach the good news
> to everyone in the world.
>
> Mark 16:15

Helping Always

Mark 16:14-20

Think

Are you a helper? How do you help your friends?
Would it be possible for you to help all the time? Why? Why
not?

Learn

It was time to say good-bye. Jesus told the disciples to tell
everyone about Him. Jesus told them that the Holy Spirit
would come soon. Then Jesus was received up into heaven.
He sat down at the right hand of God. But His job was not
finished. He helps us every day. He never stops helping.

✚ Pray

Dear Jesus, thank You for helping me. I know You are watching over me.

Christ died and was raised
to life, and now he is at God's
right side, speaking to him for us.
Romans 8:34